Other books by Matthew J. Cochran

Devotions for Disciples – Volume 1
ISBN-13: 978-0615521992

Other books from Exagorazo Pre

A Pastoral Letter to the Captives, and other works
Edited with Commentary by Vicki Claudio
ISBN-13: 978-1441417930

*Coping Through Christianity: Strengthening the Wounded
Mind and Broken Spirit Through God's Love*
by Wyatt McIntyre
ISBN-13: 978-1450501750

Journeys Through Faith
by Wyatt McIntyre
ISBN-13: 978-1450574341

Devotions for

Disciples

Who is

Jesus?

A one-month devotional guide to discovering
the second person of the Trinity

ISBN-13: 978-0615574134

ISBN-10: 0615574130

Library of Congress Control Number: 2011944620

"Consider Jesus. Know Jesus. Learn what kind of Person it is you say you trust and love and worship. Soak in the shadow of Jesus. Saturate your soul with the ways of Jesus. Watch Him. Listen to Him. Stand in awe of Him. Let Him overwhelm you with the way He is."

---John Piper

Table of Contents

Foreword

by Pastor Eddy Williams

It is a tremendous privilege for me to share with you why Matt Cochran's 30-day devotional, has special meaning for me. Matt has grown to be a great friend since he came to serve at our church and I have watched him grow so much in his relationship with Christ. Matt's heart bleeds discipleship and his focus is helping people come to know Jesus and then helping them grow in Christ. He is a rare young man.

Let me share with you about something that just happened in my life that has brought me very close to the Jesus that Matt writes so well about in this devotional. It was on October 24, 2011 at around 10 pm that I experienced a massive heart attack. I was rushed to the emergency room and they immediately began to do everything possible to save my life. After 14 hours of surgery the surgeon came out and reported to my wife Kathy that I had less than a 5% chance of making it from the operating room up to Intensive Care floor. It was during that 14 hours that our church had become aware of my situation and they began to flood into the waiting room with my wife Kathy and my grown children and they began to pray. What happened over the next 5 –7 days can only be described as miraculous!

Our church family and other Christian

friends began praying. They didn't stop praying. Every day for the first 4 or 5 days the reports from the doctors can be described best as very bad. My surgeon did not think I would survive. Every bad report was met with an army of prayer warriors at the hospital and all over the world crying out and asking Jesus to save my life. Church members were lined up and down the hallway close to my room and prayed to Jesus the Healer to save me. When my liver started to shut down they prayed for my liver. When my kidneys failed they cried to Jesus asking Him to intervene and heal my kidneys.

St. Joseph Hospital [in Tampa] has been around a long time. (I was born in St Joseph Hospital 60 years ago). They had never ever experienced so many people coming to pray for one person in the history of the hospital. Doctors and nurses in the Intensive Care floor and other employees that worked in different areas of the hospital were deeply moved by how God's people would not give up on seeing me brought back to life.

Matt Cochran as well as some other godly men from our church decided to come into my room and pray for me and anoint me with oil. This was after several days of bad reports. It was after I had died several times and I had to be brought back to life. Against all medical hope Matt anointed me with oil and they prayed for me to recover. The next day the doctors began to see improvements in my condition.

After you go through an experience like what I just went through and what our church went through it profoundly changes lives and it dramatically changes your perspective to the question "Who is Jesus?" I am overwhelmed when I think about how Jesus has changed my life and how He has changed the life of our church.

Eddy Williams
Associate Pastor, Christ Fellowship of Tampa
International Missions Board Missionary

4

Preface

Christology is often overlooked in written materials such as daily devotions. Sometimes we get caught up in how to apply topical truths from the Bible to our lives and forget that it's just as important to think about who God is and how that applies as well. When we ask the question "Who is Jesus?" the answers we come up with shape our view of the world, of our faith, of life in general.

The way we act, from the trust we put in God to the attitude we take towards His people, is affected by what we do with our knowledge of Christ. When we face hard times, it's incredibly important how we view Jesus. Even in the mundane choices of daily life, we decide based on what we think of Him. Is He our Lord, or just some teacher from thousands of years ago? Our Savior or just a symbolic sacrifice? Do we believe He is God or just look at Him as an example to follow?

We are shaped by how we answer the questions about who Jesus is. So it's my goal in this book of devotions to present to you the biblical view of Jesus, not anyone's opinion or what some scholars say about Him. This is your guide to seeing Jesus as He's presented in God's Word.

I'm going to ask you to do something as you read this daily devotional guide. Don't just read it each day and then put it down. Think about what each truth about Jesus means and how it applies to your life. Write down in the notes section what it means to you personally that Jesus is each of these things. Try to answer the questions I've asked in regards to each truth about Jesus. How does it change the way you're going to go about living today? How does it affect your faith? What can you do differently when you take a different view of the person of Jesus?

The titles and roles I've described here are not all-inclusive and I doubt if I had years to devote to the task that I could cover everything that can be said about Jesus. This is just an attempt at beginning to see Him for all that He is and all that it means. Use this as a guide toward gaining further understanding of the second person of the Trinity as you continue to study Him. I hope your awe and admiration grow for Him each day.

May God bless you as you seek more of Him.

Matthew J. Cochran
Christ Disciples Ministries

Jesus is God

John 10:30 I and the Father are one

As we start our journey to discover who Jesus is, we have to start with the foundational truth. Jesus is God. He has existed from eternity, was not created, and is in fact of the same essence as God the Father and the Holy Spirit. All three are God. Jesus' role is that of the Son, which we'll look into on a deeper level later on.

While many religious scholars and even many ordinary Christians claim that Jesus is a good teacher, a role model, or something else besides God, those views are not what Jesus said of Himself. Was He a good teacher, sure, the best. Was He a good role model, yes, He still is. But most importantly, what Jesus said about Himself was that He is God. He has the authority of God, the power of God, the knowledge of God, all of the characteristics of the perfect, eternal Creator.

When we downplay the fact that Jesus is more than a religious figure or an example for us to live by, we strip Him of His authority in our lives. We don't grant Him the honor and glory due Him and we treat Him as just another Muhammad, Buddha, or Joseph Smith. But He's so much more than that. He's fully God and fully man. No one else can make that claim.

When Jesus came to earth, God put on flesh. In

Him, the fullness of God was pleased to dwell[1] as the image of the invisible God[2] among us. In Him, God chose to reveal Himself, not merely an example or a good teacher. Himself.

Watch the video "Jesus is God" at
www.exagorazopress.com/whoisjesus/

How does this apply to your life?

Jesus is God. How does thinking about this fact impact the way you read the stories of Jesus in the Bible?

Notes:

---

1   Colossians 1:19
2   Colossians 1:15

Jesus, the Son

Galatians 4:4-7 But when the fullness of time had come, God sent forth his Son, born of woman, born under the law, to redeem those who were under the law, so that we might receive adoption as sons. And because you are sons, God has sent the Spirit of his Son into our hearts, crying, "Abba! Father!" So you are no longer a slave, but a son, and if a son, then an heir through God.

God exists eternally in the form of three equal but distinct persons: The Father, the Son, and the Holy Spirit. Often when we talk about "God" we're referring to God the Father. But how can God, who is spirit, and exists outside of time, be a father? And how can three be one? The answers to these types of questions are not easy to explain, but the Bible does help us understand.

All three persons of the Trinity have existed since before time[3]. No one gave birth to the Son, He's always existed. Not until He came to dwell on the earth as a man was He birthed of a woman, and even then by

---

3   John 1

choice. Jesus, the Father, and the Spirit are all equal, of the same substance[4]. His place as Son is not lesser than the Father, so verses like John 14:28 speak to purpose and not to rank. Jesus' purpose is to glorify the Father, just as the Spirit is to bring glory to Jesus.

Further, His place as Son gives us a picture of just how God wants us to be. God sent His only Son with the purpose that we also might become His sons, and if sons then heirs to everything Christ is entitled to. This word "sons" isn't gender related and doesn't exclude women, it does the opposite. There's power in using the word sons because traditionally sons have received a greater inheritance. By including females as His "sons", God has granted all the same rights to His riches. By accepting Christ, we became sons of God. And Jesus is the "firstborn" among us.

Watch the video "Jesus the Son" at
www.exagorazopress.com/whoisjesus/

How does this apply to your life?

Jesus' place as the Son of God puts Him in the position of heir to God's riches. If you're in Christ you've also been adopted into God's family. How does this change your expectations of God?

Notes:

---

4   John 10:30

Jesus, the Creator

John 1:3 All things were made through him, and without him was not any thing made that was made.

Jesus, the Savior of the world, the One who was sent to redeem mankind, is the Creator of mankind. How so? If there is only one God and He exists as three persons (Father, Son, Holy Spirit) and He has existed from eternity...then how is Jesus not the Creator?

The apostle John comes right out of the gates with his theology. No lineages, no birth story in a manger in Bethlehem – right to the point – Jesus is God. "In the beginning was the Word (Jesus, the logos), and the Word was with God and the Word was God." (Emphasis and parenthetical point mine) Wait, it gets even clearer: "All things were made through him, and without him was not any thing made that was made." Don't believe John? How about Paul? "For by Him (Jesus), all things were created, in heaven and on earth, visible and invisible...".[5]

How does it change your view of God to think about how the God who created us is the very same God who came to save us? Our Creator is our Redeemer. The One who holds all things together is the One who gave His life that we might be with Him. How's that for love? Does it change how you see Jesus? He's not just

---

5   Colossians 1:15

11

some baby we celebrate on Christmas or just some guy with a beard who taught good moral lessons. It all began with Him. And it all ends with Him.

How does this apply to your life?

Were you taught early on that Jesus took part in creation? If not, how does it change your reverence for Him to know that He's existed eternally and created all things? Make it a point to pay attention to God's creation today. Take note of how you view certain things in creation in light of the fact that Jesus brought them into being.

Notes:

Jesus, the King

Ephesians 1:20-21 that he worked in Christ when he raised him from the dead and seated him at his right hand in the heavenly places, far above all rule and authority and power and dominion, and above every name that is named, not only in this age but also in the one to come.

Long ago, God's people asked Him for a king to rule over them[6]. Though they were warned against such a thing, they still demanded to be ruled by a king. God granted their request, but the history of Israel is full of men who let them down, kings who couldn't live up to the expectations placed on them. Many of these men did not even follow God. But that was under the old covenant.

Today, God's people live under the new covenant of Christ. Jesus was appointed our King and His reign will never end. He will never disappoint because He is fully God. He will never lead us astray because He knows all things and He is good. He will never fail because all things have been placed under His

---

6   I Samuel 8

dominion. His kingdom will know no end. At the very name of Jesus, every knee will bow, in heaven and on earth and under the earth, and every tongue will confess that He is Lord, to the glory of God the Father[7].

He came to this earth, not to establish an earthly kingdom (though He could have), but to grant access to His heavenly kingdom – where nothing can destroy what He has created. To what king do you pledge your allegiance?

How does this apply to your life?
How much do you trust Jesus? Do you give Him full control of all aspects of your life? If not, what would it look like if you did?

Notes:

---

7   Philippians 2:10-11

14

Jesus, the Messiah

John 4:25-26 The woman said to him, "I know that Messiah is coming (he who is called Christ). When he comes, he will tell us all things." Jesus said to her, "I who speak to you am he."

For many years, God's people waited for a promised Messiah, the Chosen One whom God would send to save them and redeem them. They waited eagerly, expectantly. But when the Messiah arrived, when He was right in front of them – they didn't recognize Him.

For the Jews, the Messiah was going to be a powerful conqueror who would crash the scene and free them from their oppressors. Then he would establish his kingdom and they'd all live happily ever after. But things didn't happen that way. Jesus didn't come riding on a stallion, shooting fireballs at the Romans. No, He first came as a baby born in a stable, then He was a carpenter, then a traveling rabbi with no place to call home – a servant to those around Him.

He didn't come to be served, but to serve[8]. No wonder they couldn't recognize Him as the Messiah! But He did come to free His people – not only them but

---

8   Mark 10:45

also any who would follow after Him, Jews or otherwise. He didn't just free them from their earthly oppressors but from spiritual strongholds, from sin, from condemnation.

Whether they saw it or not, Jesus was the Messiah God had promised long ago. He conquered sin and death and His kingdom knows no end.

How does this apply to your life?

The prophecies of old concerning the Promised One were all fulfilled in Jesus. ALL OF THEM. The statistical chance of someone being capable of creating the circumstances to fake such a fulfillment is just impossible. Maybe you came to know Jesus through an emotional experience but there are others who are looking for logic. How can you show them Jesus through these fulfilled prophecies?

Notes:

Jesus, the Carpenter

Mark 6:3 "Is not this the carpenter, the son of Mary and brother of James and Joses and Judas and Simon? And are not his sisters here with us?" And they took offense at him.

Have you ever wondered what it would be like if God was just like us, trying to make a living, dealing with relationships, coping with struggles? Have you ever, like Joan Osborne, asked the question, "What if God was one of us?" The good news for us is, He was.

Jesus chose to become a man on this earth, but He didn't just show up. He chose to be born of a woman, as an infant, to grow up through childhood and, through puberty, through all of the struggles and pains that we experience. Why did He do this? He could have just showed up on a cloud in glory.

He could have done whatever He wanted, but He chose to reveal Himself in the form of a human man who lived an ordinary life like the people around Him. How does it make you feel to know that the God who has all the power to help you in your struggles has also experienced them[9]? Does it change the way you pray to know that you've never gone through anything that God

---

9   Hebrews 4:15

doesn't already know firsthand[10]?

In our despair, and even just in our normal daily struggles, we can't say that we have a God who doesn't know what it's like. He knows what all of it is like and He cares enough about us to put Himself through it for our sake.

Watch the video "Jesus the carpenter" at www.exagorazopress.com/whoisjesus/

How does this apply to your life?

Jesus lived a real life in which He was born into the world as a baby, grew up into maturity, worked a real job, ate food, hurt Himself, related with friends, and identified with people. He didn't sit on a throne where He would never know what we go through. He lived just like one of us and knows what we go through. When you're at work or school this week, what would it look like if Jesus was next to you?

Notes:

---

10 Hebrews 2:18

Jesus, the Sacrificial Lamb

John 1:29 The next day he saw Jesus coming toward him, and said, "Behold, the Lamb of God, who takes away the sin of the world!

The entire Bible is the story of Jesus. Long before He came to earth as a baby in a manger, God showed His people pictures of the future. When Abraham was set to sacrifice Isaac, a scapegoat was provided in his place[11]. When the Israelites in Egypt were preparing to flee with Moses, God had them shed the blood of a spotless lamb so that death would pass over them. Then, the perfect Lamb of God entered the scene.

All along, God had been telling the story of Jesus through the lives of His people. Then He sent His own sacrificial Lamb. But this sacrifice was good enough to cover all sins – once, and for all. Only Jesus, who lived among His creation, facing the same temptations as you and I, but without sinning, could take all of the sins of the world onto Himself. Only He could provide that sacrifice for redemption. Only He could bring justification.

John the Baptist saw it right away when he

---

11   Genesis 22:1-19

declared Jesus "the Lamb of God who takes away the sins of the world". Paul understood the symbolism when he spoke of Jesus as "our Passover lamb"[12]. Do you see Him for what He is? He bought your freedom with His life.

How does this apply to your life?

You can never be reminded too often that Jesus took on all of your sins and our guilt and put on you His own righteousness. This fact needs to stay with you all day, everyday as you remember the grace God's shown you. How can you remain conscious of this while you're going about your day?

Notes:

---

12   1 Corinthians 5:7

Jesus, the Risen Lord

Luke 24:5b-6a "Why do you seek the living among the dead? He is not here, but has risen.

Why do we look for the living among the dead? Just as those who lived with Jesus while He was on the earth, we can tend to look for Jesus in the tomb. But He's not there. Some think of Jesus with some sentimentality, as though He was once great, but now lies powerless in the grave. But He's not there. He is alive.

If Jesus was not resurrected, He would be unable to act as our intercessor today. His purpose in dying would not have fully been successful. But because He lives, He mediates between God and man. Because He lives, He has the power to act as Lord. Because He lives, the work of the cross is finished and we have redemption. Our God is not a dead god. Our God has all power and authority.

What other god ever loved his people so much that he would sacrifice his own life to save them? Who, in the history of mankind, ever sacrificed himself only to rise from the dead? Only one. Jesus Christ, the Son of God, gave His own life for us but lives now to act on our behalf. He lives so we live. If this wasn't true, our faith would be in one who was powerless to be Lord of all.

21

But He does live. He will be with us for all time. And He is Lord of all.

Watch the video "Jesus the risen Lord" at www.exagorazopress.com/whoisjesus/

How does this apply to your life?

He is alive! How could He work in your life otherwise? How could He be Lord? He lives and so you live. Have you forgotten this lately? How does it change your view of your current life situation to remember this fact?

Notes:

Jesus, the Healer

*Acts 3:6 But Peter said, "I have no silver
and gold, but what I do have I give to you.
In the name of Jesus Christ of Nazareth,
rise up and walk!"*

Many accounts are given in the New Testament
of Jesus healing people. From the blind, to the lame, to
the dead, Jesus is the ultimate physician. When He heals,
God Himself has made someone well. Of course it's
fascinating to watch events unfold as the Son of God
lays hands on the sick and brings them to health. But it's
also noteworthy that the very power of His name caused
some to be healed.

Those who had walked the earth with Jesus
knew His power. Peter, who had walked on water and
seen his Lord calm the storms, knew what Christ was
capable of. He had confidence that it was not he who
would heal the sick, but Christ's power through Him.
He claimed that power and gave it and he used it in
ministry.

The power of Christ in us can do more than heal
physical ailments. He can heal broken hearts, mend
broken relationships, reconcile sinners to God, and
regenerate hearts and lives. If there's anything that can
be broken, He can fix it. If there's anything that can
deteriorate, He can heal it. There's nothing outside His

ability as the great Healer.

How does this apply to your life?

Nothing that could affect you physically, mentally, emotionally, or spiritually is beyond the healing touch of the Savior. Read the miracle stories presented in the Gospels and ask yourself how you should be praying differently in light of the fact that Jesus is the great healer.

Notes:

Jesus, the Provider

*Philippians 4:19 And my God will supply
every need of yours according to his riches
in glory in Christ Jesus.*

There is only one who is capable of providing
for your every need. No matter what you lack, He's got
it in stock. You see, everything is His. He owns all
things. As the Psalmist put it, the "cattle on a thousand
hills" are His[13]. Since He owns everything, He's capable
of providing anything you could ever need. He lacks
nothing.

This sounds like God the Father. Yes, God the
Father does provide our every need but notice that He
gives "according to His riches in glory in Christ Jesus."
God's riches, all of His treasure, is in the glory of Jesus!
When Jesus was sent to this earth to die for our sins,
heaven was literally bankrupted of all its riches. God
put it all on the line, every chip was on the table. God's
greatest treasure to give is Himself!

Jesus is our Great Provider. Just as He supplied
endless food from just a small amount of bread and fish,
He can give us all we need. This doesn't just mean our
physical needs. What we need most is not more things,
more respect, more prestige, or more wealth. Not even

---

13 Psalm 50:10

more health! No, what we need is more of Him! He's sufficient for our lives. Everything we need is found in Jesus.

Watch the video "Jesus the provider" at
www.exagorazopress.com/whoisjesus/

How does this apply to your life?

The one you pray to for every need is also the one who owns everything! What do you need right now? Ask that your Provider would grant it.

Notes:

Jesus, the Teacher

John 13:15 For I have given you an example, that you also should do just as I have done to you.

Many people, even non-Christians, would say that Jesus was a good teacher. From the Sermon on the Mount to His parables, people love Jesus the teacher. But His best lessons weren't what He talked about, no not at all. His best lessons were taught through His example. What He chose to do shows us His priorities.

Jesus taught His disciples many things (thereby teaching us also as we can read about these lessons), but the one time He actually said that He was showing an example of something they should emulate was when He washed their feet. The one thing Jesus said to copy Him on was when He acted as a servant, showing love even to His enemy. Knowing full well that Judas Iscariot would betray Him, Jesus humbled Himself to the level of a servant before him.

All of His other teachings draw from the truth that He showed by this act – he who wants to be first has to be last. The leader must be the servant. With that in mind, the other teachings seem to have a theme.

Jesus didn't just lecture about love, He taught it through acting it out. He went so far as to demonstrate ultimate love by dying on a cross to set captives free.

He's a teacher worth learning from. He's an example worth following.

Watch the video "Jesus the teacher" at
www.exagorazopress.com/whoisjesus/

How does this apply to your life?

What can Jesus teach you today? Read a Gospel story and take note of the character of Christ. How can you learn from that example right now in this moment?

Notes:

Jesus, the Heir

Hebrews 1:2 but in these last days he has spoken to us by his Son, whom he appointed the heir of all things, through whom also he created the world.

Jesus is not just a man, not an angel, not even a god. He's THE God, heir to all things, worthy of all praise and even the worship of the angels. All things have been granted to Him. Just as a firstborn son gets an inheritance, God's Son gets the inheritance of all inheritances.

A never-ending kingdom is His, and all that's in it. His throne will know no end. He upholds the universe by the word of His power. This is His role as heir. All power and authority is His. This is a mighty thing, but Jesus shares it with us. We start out with no power and He starts out with all of it. What we have is ours because He's given it to us.

When we become children of God through faith in Christ, we become coheirs with Him[14]. What He has, we have. Power and authority are ours in His name and for His will. We have the mission that He gives us. Our commission is to reach the lost and make them disciples,

---

14 Romans 8:17

29

to teach them all that Jesus taught and to baptize them into His family in His name. The name of the Father, the Son, and the Holy Spirit.

How does this apply to your life?

There's nothing that isn't His and He doesn't keep it all to Himself. You have access to the kingdom of God through Jesus Christ. How does this empower you to share in His task of reaching the lost?

Notes:

Jesus, the Mediator

1 Timothy 2:5-6 For there is one God, and there is one mediator between God and men, the man Christ Jesus, who gave himself as a ransom for all, which is the testimony given at the proper time.

In the course of human history, many attempts have been made to reach God. People have built towers to get to heaven, invented superstitions, taken part in religious practices, called on saints, and all other sorts of things that fail to bridge the gap between God and man. None of them even come close.

The thing is, God is holy and we're sinful. We can't get into His presence in our current state. Only someone who's lived a perfect life can get to God. Because Jesus is fully God and yet lived an earthly life free from sin as a fully human man, He's the only acceptable bridge between us and God. Only He can stand between us and God and reconcile us to each other.

When we pray, our words would fall on deaf ears were it not for Jesus petitioning on our behalf. Because His righteousness has been imparted on us, God hears us when we call out to Him. We don't pray to Jesus, we pray through Him and He takes it to the Father. Without Him, we'd have no way and no chance. No saint can mediate for us. No prayer placed in a way

31

can reach God.   No amount of chanting or cutting or
burning can make our prayers effective.   Only Jesus can.
And He does.

How does this apply to your life?

There's a huge gap between God and man because of
sin.   You can't bridge the gap on your own, but
thankfully, Jesus did it for you.   Are you praying in
Jesus' name, according to His will?

Notes:

Jesus, the Redeemer

Colossians 1:13-14 He has delivered us from the domain of darkness and transferred us to the kingdom of his beloved Son, in whom we have redemption, the forgiveness of sins.

You and I were once under the wrath of God, helpless to free ourselves from the state we found ourselves in. We were enemies of God and we never could have done anything to appease Him. It was beyond our ability to reach out to Him.

But God, in an act of amazing grace, reached out to us. He extended His hand in peace by offering His Son to die in our place. His perfect, sinless Son willingly became our sin and paid the price we owed. And He set us free. He redeemed us. Do you understand the term redeemer? Do you realize the weight it carries?

A redeemer is one who buys something or someone back, say out of slavery or bondage for example. An Old Testament picture of the redeemer concept is given in the book of Ruth when Boaz redeems Ruth out of her widowhood. Jesus became our Redeemer which means He purchased us at a price. Now we belong to Him. We're His. But belonging to

Christ is where true freedom is found. It's in Him that we really find life.

No one can ever take us away from our Redeemer. Once Jesus has paid the price for us, we're His, once and for all. We can never lose Him and He'll never leave us.

How does this apply to your life?

True freedom is found only in Christ. Is anything keeping you in bondage today? Is it an addiction? A pattern of destructive thought? A relationship?

Notes:

Jesus, the Friend

John 15:15   No longer do I call you servants, for the servant does not know what his master is doing; but I have called you friends, for all that I have heard from my Father I have made known to you.

Can Jesus really be your friend? The Creator of the universe, your BFF? Well, it all depends really. The first thing that needs to be pointed out is that we do not get to decide if we're friends of Jesus. He chooses us, not the other way around[15].

Secondly, there are stipulations to being a friend of God. "If you do what I command you," He says[16]. With Christ we don't get a genie in a bottle who we can manipulate to get what we want. We get a loving God who cares about us but expects us to give our lives to Him.

Are you a friend of God? Is your whole life His? You don't get to take your ball and go home in this friendship if you don't like what you're hearing. If the Lord of all chose you as His friend, you're never going to be apart from Him. In good times and in bad, He's by

---

15 John 15:16
16 John 15:14

your side. When you need Him, He's there. When you fall, He'll pick you up. And best of all, He gave His life for you. There's no greater love than that[17].

Watch the video "Jesus the friend" at
www.exagorazopress.com/whoisjesus/

How does this apply to your life?

The Creator of all things loves you enough to befriend you. A friend wants good things for those they love and Jesus wants you to have the best thing of all. Him. Do you meet the requirement given to be called His friend?

Notes:

---

17 John 15:13

Jesus, the High Priest

Hebrews 5:5 So also Christ did not exalt himself to be made a high priest, but was appointed by him who said to him, "You are my Son, today I have begotten you"

In the days of the Old Testament priests, a sacrifice was made on behalf of the people by the High Priest. This would atone for their sins for the period of one year. In this way the priest brought God and man together. At least for that year.

Jesus is the perfect High Priest because He serves as both the priest and the sacrifice. He brings God and man together by the shedding of His own blood, not that of an animal. The sacrifice of this perfect Lamb is once and for all, not just to atone for a limited period of time. No other sacrifice ever needs to be made for the redemption of mankind. The price has been paid.

Jesus didn't appoint Himself to the position of High Priest, but He's the only one who can fill the role perfectly. Unlike all other High Priests who had to offer sacrifices for their own sins as well as those of the people, Jesus can atone for our sins by offering His own life, which is perfect, in the place of ours. And that's just what He did. Our High Priest knows all of the struggles we face and yet lived without sin. That makes

Him the only one worthy of presenting the sacrifice for our forgiveness.

How does this apply to your life?

Dwell on this idea of Jesus as High Priest. Has it ever been part of the way you think of Jesus? Why or why not?

Notes:

Jesus, the Perfect Adam

Romans 5:18 Therefore, as one trespass led to condemnation for all men, so one act of righteousness leads to justification and life for all men.

Adam, the first created man, was made to glorify God. In everything he did from having dominion over the earth to naming every animal created, Adam was meant to be an image-bearer of God. He was created in the image of God.

As you know, the story goes that Adam didn't succeed at being perfect, holy, or righteous. He, along with the first woman, Eve, introduced sin into the world. They changed the whole story. No longer could mankind live in harmony, in perfect communion with God. The direct link between God and man was broken.

But Jesus also bears the image of God. He wasn't created, like Adam, He's always been. But where Adam fell short , Jesus succeeded perfectly. Death came through Adam because he brought sin to humanity, but life came through Christ because He defeated sin and brought righteousness to humanity.

We needed one who had lived a perfect life free from sin to be our perfect sacrificial atonement for the forgiveness of our sins. Jesus is that one, the one perfect image-bearer of God. Because of Him, the image of God in us has been restored. He is the fulfillment of Adam's calling – the perfect Adam.

How does this apply to your life?
You bear the image of God because Jesus restored it. What does it mean to be an image-bearer?

Notes:

Jesus, the Perfect Isaac

Genesis 22:8 Abraham said, "God will provide for himself the lamb for a burnt offering, my son." So they went both of them together.

If you're unfamiliar with the story of Abraham and Isaac, here's the short version. Abraham was old and without any children. God promised him not only a son, but that he would father an entire nation Abraham and his wife give birth to Isaac and shortly thereafter, God asks Abraham to sacrifice his only son on an altar.

This sounds harsh, but the good news is that God provided a scapegoat (literally) to be sacrificed in Isaac's place. This is a beautiful picture of the sacrificial lamb who was to come. But when Jesus came, He was the scapegoat. He was the one who died in the place of another. As far as we know, Isaac went willingly to the altar, even though he may have been a bit ignorant of what was happening. But Jesus knew full well what was to happen to Him, and He went willingly anyway. Before He even came to earth He knew that He would die in our place, and He chose to come anyway. He fulfilled the true sacrifice that was necessary.

How does this apply to your life?

Have you ever had to give up something you loved? How willing would you be to give it up if God asked for it? Think about the fact that He gave His only Son.

Notes:

Jesus, the Perfect Moses

John 1:17 For the law was given through Moses; grace and truth came through Jesus Christ.

Long ago, God handed down the Law through His servant Moses. We know the Ten Commandments but many more rules and regulations were established for God's people – to show them how to be holy. If one could keep all of the Law, they could be righteous. The problem is, no one can keep all of the Law. The Law does not have the power to enable us to do what it says. It can guide, but its power ends there. It merely shows us where we fail.

That's where Jesus comes in. He fulfills the Law because He's perfect, but He also sets us free from the Law so that we don't have to live under its burden. Because He is righteous, we can be righteous through Him instead of through keeping the Law. In Him we have forgiveness for the times we haven't kept the Law because only one who has perfectly kept it has any right to grant that forgiveness.

His grace makes us free to obey out of love instead of obligation. In fact, the more we understand His grace the more we want to obey. The Law shows us sanctification, Jesus empowers us to achieve it. He is the fulfillment of Moses' calling – the perfect Moses.

How does this apply to your life?

Jesus came to fulfill the Law, but not to abolish it. What does this mean for you as a Christian?

Notes:

Jesus, the Perfect Jonah

Matthew 12:41 The men of Nineveh will rise up at the judgment with this generation and condemn it, for they repented at the preaching of Jonah, and behold, something greater than Jonah is here.

The story of Jonah is one of redemption. The prophet was sent to a people that God wanted to reach with His message. Jonah's dislike of the people caused him to initially refuse the assignment. But as we know, he eventually did go and the people did receive God's message of repentance through Jonah. Despite their turning their hearts toward God, however, Jonah still refused to love these people.

Contrast this with the story of Jesus, who obediently went to the people God wanted to reach. Unlike the Ninevites, these people were upright and religious. Yet they rejected Jesus' message and did not turn to Him as God. And here, unlike Jonah, Jesus chose to love them anyway. He came out of His love and He remained in His love. Then, in the ultimate act of love, He died for those who had rejected Him.

Jesus was the perfect missionary. He lived out a perfect life as an example and spoke with authority. He loved those He sought to reach. Though the people rejected Him, He fulfilled the call of Jonah, making Him the perfect Jonah.

How does this apply to your life?

Unlike Jonah, Jesus was willing to go. Which of them do you most identify with at this time in your life? Are you reluctant or eager to follow the will of God?

Notes:

Jesus, the Good Shepherd

John 10:14-15 I am the good shepherd. I know my own and my own know me, just as the Father knows me and I know the Father; and I lay down my life for the sheep.

You don't need to know them, you just need to know Him. Many Christians spend a lot of time on learning to discern spirits so that when the time comes they'll know who it is that speaks to them. They study demonology and learn all about angels so that their discernment is fine tuned to what good and evil sound like. The best thing we can do though, is learn to hear the voice of Jesus.

The Good Shepherd said that those who are of His flock know His voice, that all the rest are strangers and we'll know not to listen to them. The more time spent with Jesus, the more we'll know His voice. We won't need to practice knowing other voices so as not to listen to them, we just won't listen to them because they're not Him. Just as an infant knows his mother's voice and doesn't need to study the voices of others to know that they're not her, we can know Jesus so intimately that we know His voice better than all others.

Only one died for His flock. Jesus laid down His life for us, the Son of God sacrificing Himself that those who belong to Him would know life. He laid down His life on His own authority and He took it back up on His own authority. That's a voice worth listening to.

Watch the video "Jesus the good shepherd" at www.exagorazopress.com/whoisjesus/

How does this apply to your life?

Knowing Jesus is knowing God. To hear His voice and follow it is to do the will of God. Do you know His voice?

Notes:

Jesus, the Victorious One

1 Corinthians 15:57 But thanks be to God, who gives us the victory through our Lord Jesus Christ.

No matter what the scenario, Jesus wins. Sin? He conquers it. Death? He defeats it. Enemies? They stand no chance against the risen Son of God. He wins – period. Nothing and no one can defeat Him.

The victory of Christ translates into our own lives, though we don't always realize it and put it into practice. The enemies that we face, the trials, the temptations, the suffering – His victory bought ours. We are more than conquerors in Christ Jesus. His victory is our victory.

We can't achieve any of these victories on our own. Without the power of Christ we're utterly incapable and we'll never win over anything. But in Him we can't lose. If our goals are His goals and our desires are His desires, we're assured of victory.

Jesus not only wins in the end, He's already won. He's already triumphed over sin and death, already crushed the enemy in defeat. Nothing new can come up against Him because He's already taken on every opposition and emerged victorious. Because He won, we can win. Because of His victory, we get a prize.

How does this apply to your life?

Because His work is already accomplished, you don't need to fear failure because the battle is already won on your behalf. What battles are you in right now? Does it change your mindset about that battle to know that Jesus wins on your behalf?

Notes:

Jesus, the Word of God

John 1:1 In the beginning was the Word, and the Word was with God, and the Word was God.

Before there was anything, He was there. Before the world, before time, Jesus existed as God and with God. Nothing that we know was made without Him. He had His hand in it all – and He still does.

The ancients used to have a concept of the *Logos*, the life force that governs all things. Several religions adhered to this belief and it's no coincidence that the word used in John's Gospel to describe Jesus as the Word is *Logos*. He is the source from which all things receive life.

The *Logos* became flesh. He entered into time and put skin on for our benefit. He lived and walked among us, to complete a life lived without sin in complete righteousness. He was God's revelation of Himself to man, eating and drinking among them, feeling their pain, and laying down His own life, on His own accord.

The treasure of heaven, God's best, left and entered into His creation. He bankrupted heaven to be born a baby to a virgin mother of no wealth. The Word became a servant and showed us what love really is. Jesus was and is, in every way, God's way of showing

Himself – His character, His love, His example, His sacrifice, His forgiveness. He is God.

Watch the video "Jesus the Word of God" at www.exagorazopress.com/whoisjesus/

How does this apply to your life?

God's greatest gift is that of Himself. What might you be loving more than Him right now?

Notes:

Jesus, the Cornerstone

Luke 20:17-18   But he looked directly at them and said, "What then is this that is written: "The stone that the builders rejected has become the cornerstone'? Everyone who falls on that stone will be broken to pieces, and when it falls on anyone, it will crush him"

There comes a point in the life of every person when a choice must be made. What will we do with Jesus Christ? Will we see Him for who He is or will we discard Him and choose to make ourselves our own gods? There is no more important decision we'll ever make.

Jesus is not only the cornerstone of our faith, He is a stumbling block for those who reject Him. Eternity hinges on this one person. Either we allow Him His rightful place in our lives as Lord or we stumble over what to do with Him and we find ourselves crushed under the wrath of God.

History itself is defined by Jesus. The calendar revolves around Him, the movement He started cannot be stopped. He's the single most prolific figure who has every existed in the history of mankind and when He returns, this world as we know it comes to an end. It's all about Him.

Whatever we may think this life is all about, we're wrong unless we consider Jesus the dividing line. Where we stand on the matter of who He is makes every difference in the world. So what have you done with Christ? Is He the cornerstone of your faith or the stumbling block in your path?

How does this apply to your life?

Is your foundation built upon Jesus? What does this mean for you? How would you describe it to someone else?

Notes:

Jesus, the Light of the World

John 8:12 Again Jesus spoke to them, saying, "I am the light of the world. Whoever follows me will not walk in darkness, but will have the light of life."

"Let there be light." These words were spoken and so it all began. Time and all that exists came to be only after this one sentence brought about the beginning. And then, in the course of human history, the true Light came into the world. The one who spoke light into being was the true Light, and in Him all can be enlightened[18].

Just as we stumble around in the darkness for lack of light, we stumble around in our sin, lost in it, without the Light of the World. If we walk with Jesus, we will never walk in darkness because He'll guide us. He'll be the lamp to our feet and the light to our path[19].

Also, if we walk with Jesus we'll ourselves be light to the world[20]. In us, the world will see Him. They'll find hope in Him, they'll see His love. Our lives will bear witness to the One who sent us, just as His life

---

18 John 1:9
19 Psalm 119:105
20 Matthew 5:14

bore witness to the One who sent Him[21].

Let His light shine through you. Others may see it and turn to Him[22].

How does this apply to your life?

Jesus told His disciples that they were also the "light of the world", a "shining city on a hill". If you're walking in the light, how does this look to others? How would they describe what they see in you?

Notes:

---

21 John 8:18
22 Matthew 5:16

Jesus, the Way

John 14:6 Jesus said to him, "I am the way, and the truth, and the life. No one comes to the Father except through me.

Today we like to think we're very enlightened, so much more educated than the ancients. We think we're bright enough to pick and choose aspects of different religions, tailoring our belief system, and we think this is some new thought. Actually, the pagans of centuries ago saw no problem with pledging allegiance to multiple deities from different backgrounds until they found what suited them.

Jesus was clear though when He spoke of the way to God. Only He can serve as that bridge. Only through belief on Him can we see heaven. He is the only way. We can try out custom-made religions, but in the end they're empty, devoid of any true meaning. Christ has the answer.

By God's grace we're saved; we can't do anything to earn our way to Him. But He extended this grace in the offering of His Son on our behalf for the forgiveness of sins. This action by God just shows how He expects us to be reconciled to Him. Only through Jesus. And only means only.

Watch the video "Jesus the way" at
http://www.exagorazopress.com/whoisjesus/

How does this apply to your life?

If you had the cure for cancer, you'd share it. What are you doing to tell others about the one Way to God?

Notes:

Jesus, the Truth

John 14:6 Jesus said to him, "I am the way, and the truth, and the life. No one comes to the Father except through me.

What is truth? The question has been asked through the ages. Even Pontius Pilate, with the Son of God standing before Him, posed the question. So often we're like Pilate, asking what truth is when it's standing right in front of us. Truth doesn't exist outside of God. Jesus is truth in the form of a man.

No one has ever spoken nothing but the complete truth their entire life except for Christ. No matter how hard we may try, we all speak untruth from time to time, even when it's not intentionally. But not one word that ever came from the mouth of Jesus was false. If He said it, we can believe it.

So what did He say? He said He was God[23]. He said He would rise from the dead[24]. He said He had all power and authority[25]. Now we either believe Him in all of it or we believe none of it. There is no in-between. If we say He was a good teacher but discredit Him as the Son of God, we have to look past the fact that He claimed Himself to be God. If He claimed to be God but

---

23 John 10:30
24 Matthew 20:19
25 Matthew 28:18

wasn't, that isn't a good teacher...that's a liar.

The source of truth is God. His goodness testifies to truth and there is only truth in Him. He can't lie[26]. If He says it, it's worth believing.

Watch the video "Jesus the truth" at
www.exagorazopress.com/whoisjesus/

How does this apply to your life?

The world's idea is truth is that it's relative. It's easy to get sucked into that. Assess yourself. Are you really living like there are absolute truths found in Jesus?

Notes:

---

26 Numbers 23:19

Jesus, the Life

John 11:25-26 Jesus said to her, "I am the resurrection and the life. Whoever believes in me, though he die, yet shall he live, and everyone who lives and believes in me shall never die. Do you believe this?"

Are you dead? We all die at some point, but some of us die before others, some of us give up our lives and die while we still live. Is this confusing? We're all destined to die in our earthly bodies, bound for eternity either in heaven with God or hell apart from Him. But those who live in Christ have already died to themselves (in spirit) and taken on Christ's life. That's why we say we "live in Him". It's why Paul wrote of us dying to sin, dying to our old nature, etc. We've taken on a new life in Christ, we're "hidden in Him"[27]. Eternal life, for those who are in Christ, has already begun while still living on the earth.

Jesus said that He is the only way to God[28]. He also stated that He came to give life[29]. But the core truth behind this is that He is life and that's how He's able to offer it to us. Sin equals death, Jesus equals life. We

---

27 Colossians 3:3
28 John 14:6
29 John 10:10

61

choose one or the other, there are no other choices. Sin doesn't mean doing bad things, it means having an unrighteous nature. But following Christ brings onto us His nature and therefore we die to the sinful one.

He is the resurrection (the way to heaven), and the source of eternal life. If we're in Him, we'll never die (in the sense that those who spend eternity in hell "die" apart from Him). It all rests in Him, everything here and now and everything that comes after this. It begins with Him[30] and it ends with Him[31].

Watch the video "Jesus the life" at
www.exagorazopress.com/whoisjesus/

How does this apply to your life?
Before Jesus, you were dead spiritually. How does your life look different now than it did before you knew Jesus?

Notes:

---

30 John 1:1
31 Revelation 22:12-13

Jesus, the I Am

*John 8:58 Jesus said to them, "Truly, truly,
I say to you, before Abraham was, I am."*

What do you think about Jesus? Is He merely a good teacher? The Son of God? Do you think of Him as only having existed for a few decades on the earth? Let me put it to you this way; how much thought have you put into the fact that Jesus has existed from before time's existence?

Jesus did not come into existence when a baby was born in Bethlehem of Judea under an unusual star. This was the time God chose to manifest Himself in the person of Christ to mankind, but Jesus was always in existence. He is the One who was and is, and is yet to come. All things were created by Him, through Him, and for Him[32], and by Him all things hold together[33]. He's much more than a man who ministered on the earth for a few short years and then died.

Before the world was created, He knew you. Before time came into being, He knew what day you would be born and what day you would die. He knew before He created anyone exactly who would be king, ruler, President, Prime Minister, Emperor, teacher, preacher, janitor, driver, or inventor.

---

32 Colossians 1:16
33 Colossians 1:17

63

Take some time to think about Jesus beyond the normal thoughts of Him as a baby or as dying on the cross. Think about His role in creation and His role in all of history. Think about what it means that all things hold together in Him and then look all around you at the things He's holding together. Shiver in awe as you ponder the words "Before Abraham was, I am." And then worship Him and give Him glory.

Watch the video "Jesus the I Am" at
www.exagorazopress.com/whoisjesus/

How does this apply to your life?
What do you think of Jesus? What will you do with Him?

Notes:

Jesus, the Alpha and the Omega

Revelation 22:13 "I am the Alpha and the Omega, the first and the last, the beginning and the end."

It all starts with Him, the King of Kings and Lord of Lords. Jesus is the great I AM, the Alpha and the Omega. He was from the beginning, even before there was time and He holds time in His hands. It all revolves around Him. And it all ends when He says it ends.

There's been a lot of talk for many centuries about when the end times will come. Formulas have been developed, codes supposedly deciphered. Foolish men have taken a guess at when the end will come and their days have come and gone with no event. But it's not up to them to determine when Christ will return.

When the end of this age comes, we will know it because the Messiah will once again reveal Himself to mankind, but this time it will be with a different purpose. When the end comes we will know it because it will all revolve around Christ and His majesty. It's not about a collision between the earth and an asteroid or even global warming. At the appointed time (that only the Father knows), Christ will return for His bride and all things will be made new. It won't be about what could have happened or when it did happen, it will be about

Him.

It all began with Him and it all ends with Him, when He says so. Christ's return will be an event that no one will miss, no matter where they are in the world. Every eye will be on Him and every knee will bow before Him. At that time everyone will know who the great I Am is and they'll confess Him as Lord.

How does this apply to your life?

"Surely I am coming soon", the words of Christ, can be trusted. We don't know when He will return for us but we do know that He will return. He will come in His time and not until then. Are you ready? What does it mean to be ready?

Notes:

Jesus, the Hope

Romans 8:38-39   For I am sure that neither death nor life, nor angels nor rulers, nor things present nor things to come, nor powers, nor height nor depth, nor anything else in all creation, will be able to separate us from the love of God in Christ Jesus our Lord.

The Bible, God's Word, is about Jesus. From the creation story in Genesis to the end of all things in Revelation, God has revealed Himself through His Word and the hope that He has given mankind through redemption in Christ. He has shown that there is no other way to reconciliation with Him but through Jesus. There is only one way to God and there is only one hope for all of mankind.

Jesus is the one hope that we have for forgiveness. The one hope we have for peace. The one hope we have for eternal life with God. The only hope for salvation. It's in Him that we find rest, in Him that we find freedom and only in Him that we can find hope. Without Him there is darkness and sorrow. There is not hope apart from Him.

But, oh the hope we have in Him! In Him we are more than conquerors! Nothing, not anything on this earth or anything above this earth or below it, can separate us from the love of God that we have in Christ Jesus! That is hope. That is good news.

And we have hope in Him that this life is not the end. When Christ returns, all things will be made new. Our bodies will be new and glorious and we'll have true fellowship with each other and with God. Come, Lord Jesus, come!

Watch the video "Jesus the hope" at
www.exagorazopress.com/whoisjesus/

How does this apply to your life?
Nothing else can satisfy. Nothing else can give us life. Nothing else can stand on its own as truth. Only Jesus can satisfy. Only He can truly give life. He is truth, and when you know the truth, it will set you free. Are you free? Is your hope in Him or in other things?

Notes:

About the author:

Matt Cochran's passion is seeing people's lives transformed by a relationship with Jesus Christ. At Christ Fellowship of Tampa, Matt helps people take the Next Steps in their spiritual journey. With his daily devotions at devotionsfordisciples.com, he offers a guide in that journey.

Having served in the Marine Corps in locations all over the world, Matt easily connects with people. He holds a Bachelor's Degree in Christian Studies and is working on a Master's Degree in Discipleship Ministries at the time of this book's publishing. Matt is married to the love of his life, Rose, and they have two sons, Colin and Hank.

www.ingramcontent.com/pod-product-compliance
Lightning Source LLC
Chambersburg PA
CBHW060142050426
42448CB00010B/2257